Carving a Bear in Soapstone

Tasha Unninayar and Lynn Bartlett.
Artist, Dawn Hartwig

4880 Lower Valley Road · Atglen, Pennsylvania 19310

*I'm going to steal this
yack off you are
day for sure!
I expect a bear
for christmas.
Em.*

Other Schiffer Books by the Author:
Introduction to Soapstone Sculpting. ISBN: 9780764337819. $29.99
Carving a Coyote in Soapstone. ISBN: 978-0-7643-4009-3. $16.99

Other Schiffer Books on Related Subjects:
Carving in Soap. Howard K. Suzuki. ISBN: 0764312928. $12.95

Schiffer Books are available at special discounts for bulk purchases for sales promotions or premiums. Special editions, including personalized covers, corporate imprints, and excerpts can be created in large quantities for special needs. For more information contact the publisher:

Published by Schiffer Publishing Ltd.
4880 Lower Valley Road
Atglen, PA 19310
Phone: (610) 593-1777; Fax: (610) 593-2002
E-mail: Info@schifferbooks.com

For the largest selection of fine reference books on this and related subjects, please visit our website at
www.schifferbooks.com
We are always looking for people to write books on new and related subjects. If you have an idea for a book, please contact us at
proposals@schifferbooks.com

This book may be purchased from the publisher.
Include $5.00 for shipping.
Please try your bookstore first.
You may write for a free catalog.

In Europe, Schiffer books are distributed by
Bushwood Books
6 Marksbury Ave.
Kew Gardens
Surrey TW9 4JF England
Phone: 44 (0) 20 8392 8585; Fax: 44 (0) 20 8392 9876
E-mail: info@bushwoodbooks.co.uk
Website: www.bushwoodbooks.co.uk

Designed by RoS
Type set in SquireD/Humanist 521 BT

ISBN: 978-0-7643-4084-0
Printed in China

Acknowledgments

We would like to first thank our publisher for the opportunity to share the medium of soapstone carving in another great book and thank you to Hobby Lobby for supplying the materials and supplies. For *Carving a Bear in Soapstone*, we selected a very talented sculptor as our featured artist, Dawn Hartwig. Her years of experience and talent show in even the most basic of projects and we are just thrilled to share with you her techniques and approach. Thank you Dawn for working with us on another project. We would like to thank our dear friends and family, who have encouraged us through this process. We hope that you will find as much inspiration in carving this standing bear as we have. Happy Carving!

Authors
Tasha Unninayar and Lynn Bartlett

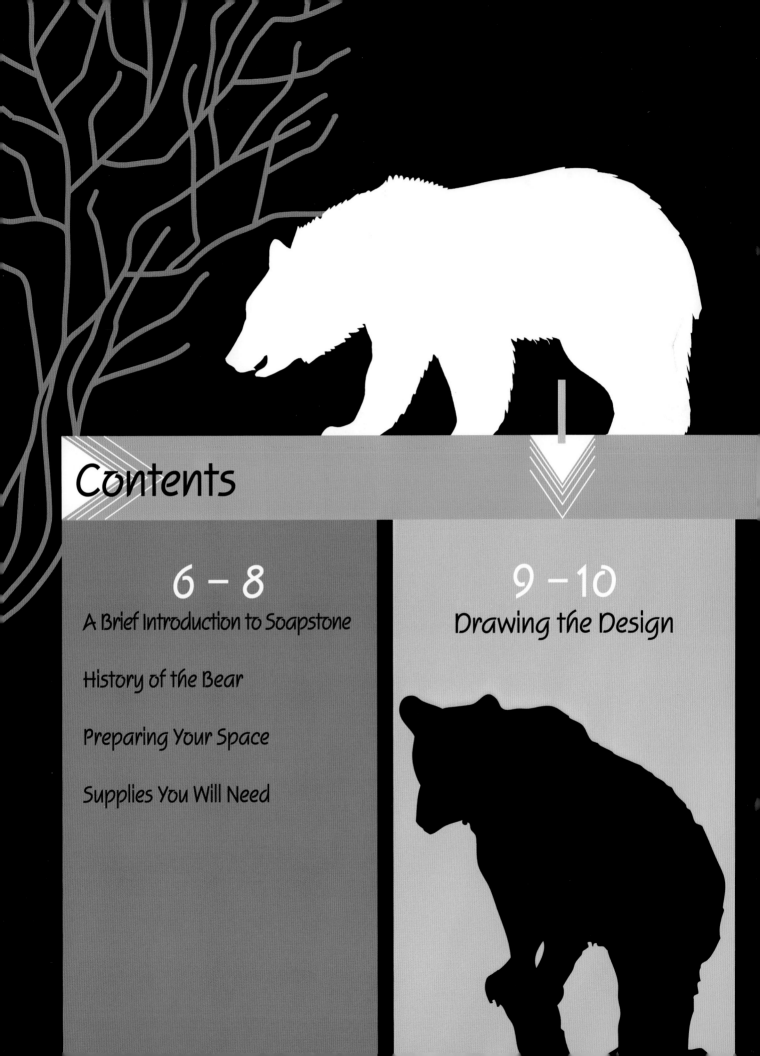

Contents

6 – 8

A Brief Introduction to Soapstone

History of the Bear

Preparing Your Space

Supplies You Will Need

9 – 10

Drawing the Design

11 – 37
Carving the Bear

Defining the Basic Shape ...12
Shaping the Waist and the Belly ...14
Defining the Profile of the Head ...16
Blocking the Head ...18
Shaping the Head and Shoulders ...20
Shaping the Legs ...24
Creating the Tail ...26
Smoothing the Body ...30
Shaping the Snout ...32
Creating the Ears ...34
Last Minute Touch Ups ...36

38 – 46
Finishing and Polishing

Sanding ...39
Polishing ...44

Bear Pattern ...47

Gallery ...48

A Brief Introduction to Soapstone

There are many materials available with which sculptors may create, such as wood, clay, marble, alabaster, and soapstone. Soapstone has always been a favorite because of its softness and ease to sculpt and manipulate. New sculptors of any age and skill level can easily accomplish fun projects with soapstone. This positive reinforcement encourages them to continue creating and learning this craft.

The art of carving stone gives you a special feeling of creating something that will last forever, perhaps even be a part of history. Your piece may become a family heirloom. There are many techniques that you can learn, ranging from techniques using electric tools found at your local hardware store to ancient techniques passed down for generations. The best part is that you don't need much to accomplish your bear. You can do it at home, in the garage, in a classroom or any comfortable space of your choosing.

White marble in raw form, wood block, golden soapstone in raw form, and clay.

History of the Bear

The bear can be found as a symbol of strength in the mythology and folklore of many cultures around the world. For instance, the Celts and the Vikings have legends concerning the strength, protectiveness, and prowess of bears, as do the Native Americans, Japanese, and Chinese. Countless myths and legends record a sort of intimacy between human beings and bears. The Koreans, for example, traditionally believe that they are descended from a bear.

Photo of a standing bear sculpture.

Preparing Your Space

Old towel, small box, old tray, and newspaper.

Hopefully you are lucky enough to be able to work outdoors on your projects, leaving the debris easy to clean up. If this is the case, find a table that you can work on (one that does not strain your back). Using lots of newspaper, cover your table in layers that you can remove as dust accumulates. If you put a wet towel under your soapstone project, you can trap the dust and discard it as you go by rinsing out the towel. You can create a "sandbag" out of an old pair of blue jeans. Cut a leg into a section and stitch one end. Fill the leg with silica sand (do not over stuff the leg), stitch the other end—bingo you have a wonderful place to work your stone.

If you are forced to work indoors, you can use a kitty litter box, or small box, and fill it with silica sand (purchased at the hardware store—they refer to it as Play Sand) half way. This box will now act as both a cushion for your piece to be worked on, as well as collect the dust.

Supplies You Will Need

Finished Round Bear.

For your bear, you will need: a piece of soapstone, in this case we used a precut stone in the bear design (you can purchase the stone precut at most suppliers or request your supplier to cut it to size, and/or cut it yourself). You can also use a raw piece of stone or a block of stone that you cut down to the basic shape. In this project we used a rasp, a four-sided file, and a flat chisel. However, the project can be accomplished with a mere rasp, but this process would take quite a bit more time and effort. You will also need a pencil, sandpaper (beginning with 80 grit, 120 grit, and 220 grit), steel wool (optional), and some olive oil, or spray lacquer for the finish. Optional supplies are a plastic mat to set the piece on, a plastic box, newspaper or old towel to catch the debris from the filing.

Raw soapstone, blocked stone, and a precut bear design.

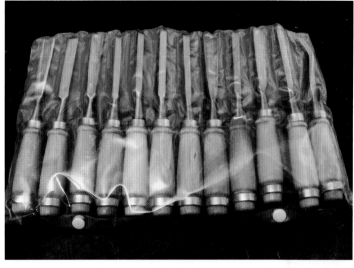

An example of a chisel set, but you can use any type of flat chisel.

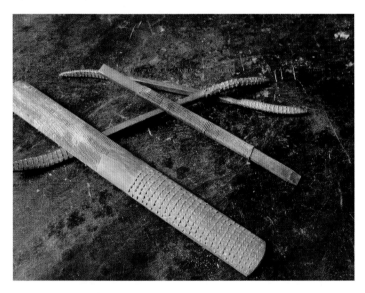

Flat four sided file, chisel, and rasps.

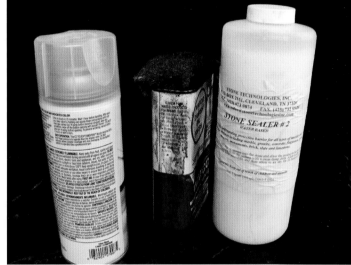

Spray lacquer, sealer, and polish.

Old towel, small box, old tray, newspaper.

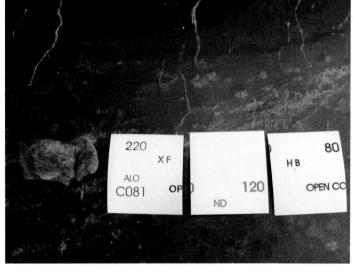

80, 120, and 220 grit sandpaper and 0000 steel wool.

You can use the project pattern or draw the design freehand. In this case, we drew the design freehand on the stone. At any time during the creation of your sculpture, we encourage you to look ahead at the photos so that you can see the process before you execute any of the steps.

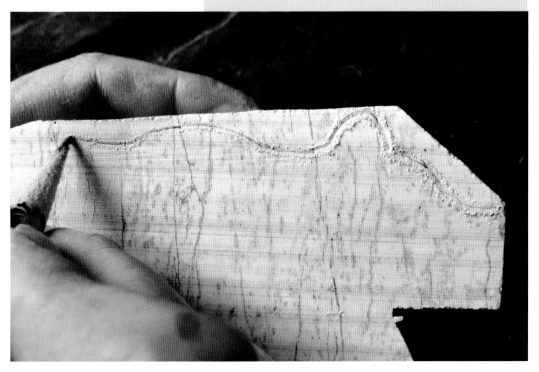

Take your precut piece of soapstone and place it in your hands so that the head and nose are facing to the right. Pick up your pencil and begin drawing the design.

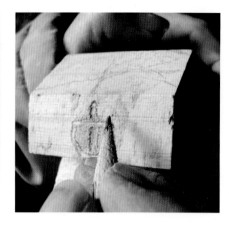

Take your piece and begin with a centerline down the middle of the top, making sure the line goes all the way down to the edge of the back.

Face the bear towards you and continue the centerline down the middle of the face. At the desired height, put in the line for the top of the paws.

With the piece still facing towards you, draw in bottom of the snout, remembering to stay in the middle of the piece by following your centerline. At the desired height, add in the line for the top of the nose.

From the side, draw in the profile of the head, add in the ear, draw in the back line, and shape the back end.

Finish at the back edge.

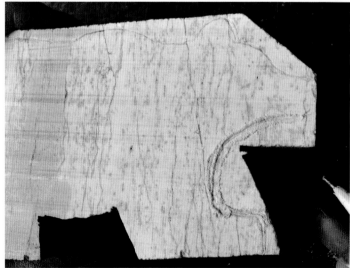

Turn the bear facing away from you and draw the tail. Remember to use your centerline for symmetry.

Face the bear to the right and draw in the lines for the paw. Draw in the chest line, following it up to the jaw.

In this chapter you will be using a flat file to remove material to define the basic shape of the standing bear. If you do not have a flat file, you can use any type of rasp. The flat file, however, is recommended.

Defining the basic shape of the standing bear.

Defining the Basic Shape

Pick up your flat file and begin filing the chest area. At any time, we encourage you to look ahead at the photos.

With the round side of the file down, use a back and forth filing motion to remove the material. File along the top of the paws to the other side of the piece.

Bring your attention to the top of the piece.

Begin filing back and forth, removing material. Here you are marking the stone for the placement of the back of the ears, so file lightly. Pause and take a look, making sure that there is enough space to create the ears.

Once satisfied with the placement, begin filing deeper. After a few strokes, begin rounding off the edge. Work the line to the other side. Don't apply too much pressure; you can always go back and remove more material. Let the motion shape the piece.

Your piece should look something like this at this stage.

Continue rounding off the edge towards the back of the bear. You can also use the flat side of the file for a more even result. It is good to pause a moment to evaluate your progress. Removing material slowly is the ideal method. Work slowly in stages, remembering that you can always remove more material but you cannot put it back! In this case, we are pausing again to identify how much rounder we want the shape of the bear. After taking a look, we decided to continue shaping the bear.

We are now working on the second pass removing material in a symmetrical way, never forgetting the centerline.

At this stage your bear should look something like this. The basic shape of the bear is beginning to take form.

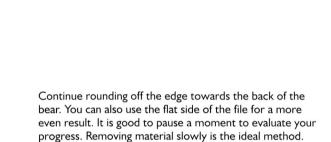

Shaping the Waist and Belly

In this section you will be creating the shape of the waistline and belly of the bear.

Shaping the waist and belly of the bear.

Place the bear on its side, in this case facing left, and draw in a line from the crease of the back of the front leg up to the desired depth of the belly area. Repeat in front of the rear leg.

Using a rasp, begin removing material, focusing on one corner. File along the line you just drew. File the other corner as well, working your way into the middle.

Begin lightly rounding the top of the back, the width of the belly, and the middle of the belly. Remember to look ahead at the photos at any time.

Make a few more passes, rounding the top of the back. Experiment with different rasp positions. Now, take a break and evaluate your piece. It should look something like this.

On the opposite side, we are starting at the top of the back and moving down, but you can repeat the same process by starting at the crease and moving up. Remember to draw lines on this side of the bear in the approximate position you did on the reverse. File down to the crease of the leg, removing material to form the belly area. File the other side of the crease, working your way into the middle of the belly. Shape the middle of the belly area. Then, slowly work your way to the top of the back. Notice the focus on the middle area above the belly. Pause and take a look at your piece. It should look something like this.

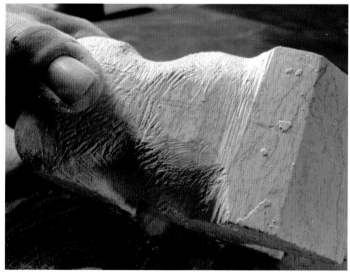

Now flip the piece over and begin shaping the underbelly.

Continue rounding the belly in general on both sides to achieve even symmetry.

Defining the Profile of the Head

In this section you will be defining the profile of the head of your bear.

Defining the profile of the head of the bear.

Begin with the piece flat on its side and file behind the ears. File in a rocking motion going from behind the ear to under the chin. Notice the slight curve of the file line forming the basic shape of this side of the head and neck area.

Shape the jaw and tip of the nose. Your piece should look something like this.

Now begin drawing in the profile of the snout. In this case we are drawing it freehand, but you can choose to use the pattern. Close up of the lines defining the ear and eye ridge. Slope the line down from the eye to the nose. Your piece should look something like this. Repeat the lines on the other side.

Take your round rasp and place it on the top of the forehead in front of the ear following your line. You will be creating the front of the ear and forehead.

File in a back and forth motion until you reach the desired depth. Work slowly as the material is being removed.

On this side of the bear, repeat shaping the jaw and neck area.

Your piece should look something like this. The head is looking more defined with the profiled outlined, the waist and belly area have more definition, and you begin to see the ears emerging.

Blocking the Head

Here you will see the shape of the head emerge.

Blocking the head of the bear.

You can use the pattern to draw the lines of the head or draw them freehand. In this case we chose to draw them freehand. Begin with the line on the right side of the piece. Start at the ear and draw forward to the snout. Repeat on the other side. Note the symmetry on either side of the centerline.

Go back over your lines when you are satisfied with their placement. Get your flat file, round side down and begin slowly removing material around the lines. Go very slowly, without too much pressure.

File parallel to the outside line.

Stop before you get too close to the line. File a little closer from a different angle near the snout. Again, work slowly. Stay just outside of the line.

Repeat on the other side. Being careful when working on the second side, it is best to proceed with continued caution. Remember, you can always take away more, but you cannot easily put it back.

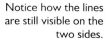
Notice how the lines are still visible on the two sides.

Shaping the Head and Shoulders

In this section, you will be defining the shape of the head and shoulders.

Shaping the head and the shoulders of the bear.

Start by putting the bear on its side. Using the flat file, gently round under the tip of the snout. Round the line all the way to the neck.

At this stage, if need be, draw back in the outline of the head. Make sure the line is dark enough. Your line should look like this and repeat on the other side. Always keep the centerline in mind.

Using a rasp, file out the slope of the snout. Remember it is critical to work slowly in this delicate area.

Here we are working on the jaw area.

Notice the roundness of the head is beginning to emerge. Using the rasp, round the chest area down to the legs. Your piece should look something like this, with the chest is getting rounder, as well as the jaw line.

At this stage of the shaping, work on several areas a little bit at a time. Work on the area behind the ears, shape the leg and paw area, behind the legs, the chest, and repeat on the opposite side.

With the rasp, begin softly rounding the top of the head.

File, slowly, in a brushing motion.

Notice the directions of the file marks and the subtle amount of material that was removed, narrowing the head. You want to work very slowly to avoid removing too much.

Continue working on the head. Watch as the shape of the head begins to emerge. Notice the difference between the two sides. Always remember to have a firm grip on your piece while working on the head or any delicate area.

You can work on the underside of the chin with a rasp, or you can use the round side of a flat file, as you see here.

Your piece at this stage should look something like this.

Flip the bear over and grab a rasp. Work on shaping the shoulder. In a delicate brushing motion, shape the lines of the legs. Repeat on the other side.

Your bear should be getting rounder and have softer lines. Both sides of the piece are being worked on at more or less the same rate. This is important to achieve symmetry.

Using the rasp in an up and down motion, slowly begin rounding the eye area. Repeat on the other side.

Notice how the eye area is becoming more apparent.

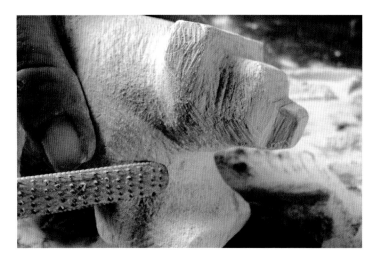

Begin slowly rounding the face and under the chin. Move down towards the shoulders in a brushing motion.

Your piece should look something like this. Notice how the front of the bear is totally softened. The angles are no longer apparent.

Shaping The Legs

This section focuses on shaping the legs of the bear. Up until now we have focused on softening the angles and now we will add definition.

Shaping the legs of the bear.

In a brushing motion, brush down under the chin, rounding as you go down to the paws. Brush up to the shoulder area.

Notice the definition behind the ear is now more apparent.

Shift your focus to the middle of the back above the front leg. In a slight twisting motion, brush the rasp towards the front leg then sweep the rasp down the leg rounding off the corner edge. Move on and begin defining the back leg as well.

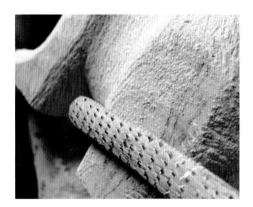

Round the edges of the back leg, using a gentle "see-saw" motion.

Deepen the definition of the crease which creates the hip of the bear.

Go back to the other side and work on rounding the edges underneath the bear. Use the light brushing technique or "see-saw" motion on the angles. In this case, we used a brushing motion down the side.

Take a moment to look at your piece and evaluate where you are and how you want to proceed. Observe how the flat panels have drastically reduced in size and the legs are more defined. Now focus on adding more definition to the high leg area. The curved rasp is a good choice for this area. The curve of the rasp is creating the curve of the leg.

At this stage, don't be afraid to pause frequently. Step back and think about what the next step will be. Using a rasp, in a back and forth motion, continue to round the hind leg.

Now using the flat rasp, round the back of the front paws. Again, you are working on the piece as a whole to achieve an even look. Round the front top of the paws.

Creating the Tail

We are focusing on the tail of the standing bear. While it may seem like a simple part of this sculpture, it is important to take your time with it.

Creating the tail of the standing bear.

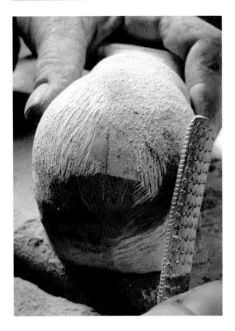

First address rounding the back of the bear using a rasp. Keep the centerline in mind and round to the desired shape.

Get your pencil and go over the "V" of the tail. Remember the symmetry on either side of the centerline. With your pencil, create a good indentation. Repeat on the other side.

Now using the tip of your pointed rasp, use the lines as a guide and gently remove material on the outside of the line. The indentation becomes deeper with the rasp. Blow away the dust periodically to see your work. From the tip of the tail, create a crevice down the piece. You should have half a "Y".

It may be easier to hold the piece upside down to do the other side. Create the crevice on this side. Here you can really begin to see the legs and the tail emerging. Blow away the dust to see the "Y".

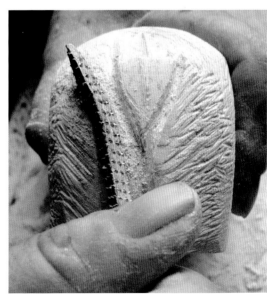

Continue to remove the stone around the tail. Remove the stone in a motion that goes away from the tail (as opposed to towards the tail).

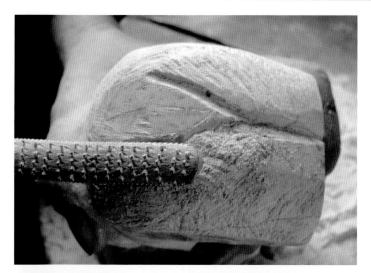

At this point you can use a different rasp to remove material more easily.

When removing material from this area, keep in mind the curve of the back of the bear. If you remove too much from any one spot you will get a "flat spot" so work all over the piece evenly. In essence you are rounding while removing the material. The tail begins to emerge while the leg is rounding. Continue working the rump.

Again, the technique is a brushing sweep with the rasp away from the tail.

Begin on the other side. If you have a pointed rasp, you can use it around the tail to achieve more depth. Your piece should look something like this.

Work on removing the material outside the crevices. Here, work from the base of the sculpture in a sweeping motion, upward, following the curvature of the tail line.

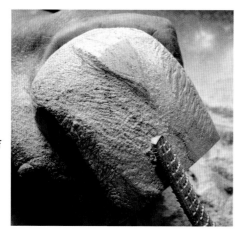

Notice the rasp marks and their directionality.

While the basic shape is achieved, continue rounding and removing material for greater depth. This will give the tail more dimension. Remember to work away from the tail. As you work around the rump, the tail begins to stand out and you can see areas that need addressing, such as the right hip side next to the tail.

In a brushing motion, work on the top area of the tail. This is to blend the tail into the base of the back.

Go down the back of the leg in a brushing motion, away from the tail on both sides. Now that you have defined the tail and the back of the legs, begin shaping the tail. Once again, work very slowly here. You will see here that the tail has not lost any thickness, but is smoother and rounder. When working on the tip of the tail, go very slowly.

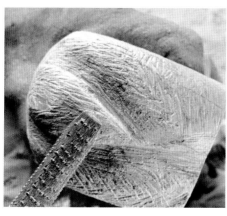

Now take some time to smooth out the hind quarters. Again keeping in mind the general symmetry of the bear. Use gentle brushing motions. Your bear should look like this.

Smoothing the Body

This section focuses on smoothing the areas that have already been defined.

Smoothing the body of the standing bear.

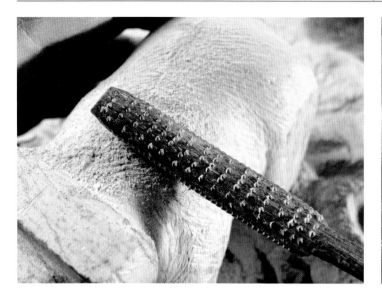

Begin working the top of the shoulders, smoothing the surface.

Move on to smoothing the legs, rounding the surface with delicate brush strokes, smoothing away the rasp marks, and following the shape of the standing bear.

The flat stone begins to round and the leg appears. Work on areas that you are not satisfied with at this stage.

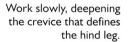

Work slowly, deepening the crevice that defines the hind leg.

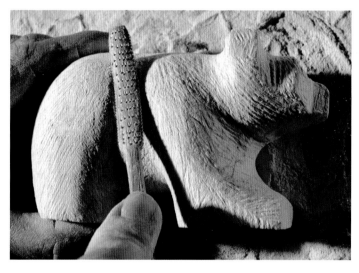

Notice the now clearly defined hind leg.

Shaping the Snout

Now, we will focus on shaping the snout of the standing bear. When working on this area, it is critical that you have a firm grip on the piece and work very slowly. Let the rasp do the work, do not apply too much pressure to the stone. It is always possible to remove more material, but nearly impossible to put back.

Shaping the snout of the standing bear.

Take at your piece and determine where the centerline is located. Draw the centerline back in if necessary, keeping in mind the symmetry of the piece and the location of the ears, eyes, and nose. Draw in the side of the snout, repeating on the other side.

Make sure the lines are clear and the line is evenly in the middle.

With your rasp, begin gently removing material from the outside of the line on the tip of the snout. Make sure you have a firm grip and are not applying a lot of pressure. Begin rounding the area. Just a few strokes will shape the snout.

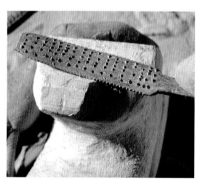

In a upward brushing motion, gently smooth and shape the head area behind the snout. Follow the curve around the snout. Pause frequently when working in detailed areas. Notice the difference between the sides. Repeat the motion for more definition. Wrap around gently to the top.

Notice the progress. Close up.

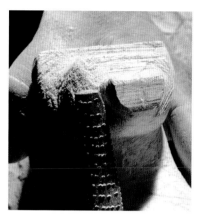

Now repeat on the other side, starting at the base of the snout. Work slowly around the head, rounding over the top of the snout. Keeping in mind your grip on the piece. Continue rounding and shaping.

At this stage, the bear should look something like this. You can really see the sweeping motions around the snout and the head.

In preparation for the ears, in a rocking motion, define the shoulders. Be sure to stay behind the delicate ears.

Creating the Ears

This section is dedicated solely to creating the ears of your bear. Remember, this is the area with the least amount of soapstone material with which to work. Therefore, it is imperative that you work slowly and carefully with a firm grip. Pause frequently and look ahead at the photos.

Creating the ears of the standing bear.

Begin by observing the centerline on the top of the ears and darken if necessary. Make sure you can see the curved outer lines as well.

Take your rasp and place it on the centerline. Gently go back and forth, separating the ears. Go slowly, letting the rasp motion remove the material, not pressure.

Now gently begin…

…rounding the base of the ear.

Blow away the dust and slowly begin to shape the ear. Notice the round curvature of the back of the ear. Notice the small indentations on the front of the ear, created with the rasp. Take the rasp and round the top left corner just a touch.

Observe the rounded ear on the left and the difference between the two.

Take your rasp and begin working on the other ear, starting at the back and rounding slowly, shaping the ear from a block to a curve.

Continue shaping the interior of the ear, following the model of the other ear. Gently brush the outside of the ear until you are satisfied with the shape.

Start at the top of the ear; take the curve down the jaw line.

A view from the top, you can see the back of the ears are evenly proportioned. Your bear should look something like this.

Last Minute Touch Ups

At this stage, you could go on to finishing the bear. However, you cannot spend enough time addressing the details of any sculpture. So, before you begin finishing the bear, take the time to go back over the entire piece, making sure that the contour is exactly what you want. We even recommend taking a break and returning to the piece with fresh eyes.

Last minute touch ups of the standing bear.

Take a look at the head—we chose to touch up the side of the ears.

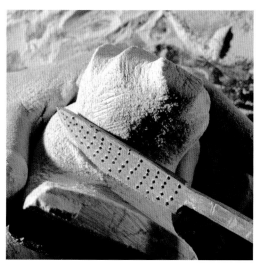

Looking at the chest, we needed some additional smoothing.

Take a look at the jaw line. Look at the piece from all angles. You are looking for uneven symmetry, lumps and oddities. Smooth out any flaws you see.

Brush away any deep tool marks. Last minute chance to make alterations!

Pause and look at your piece. Your bear should look something like this.

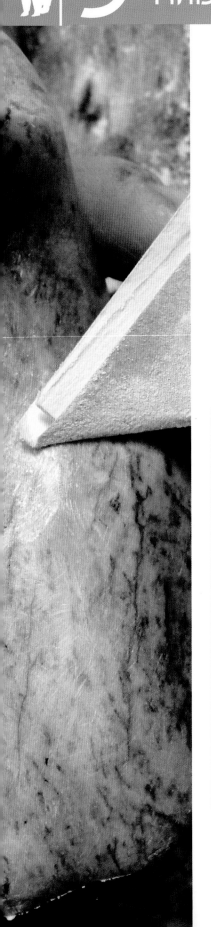

Now you will be sanding the standing bear. You will need some sandpapers; we use 80, 120 and 220 grit sandpapers in this project, but you can go up to 800 grit if you choose. The finer the grit, the smoother the polish. This stage of the project is perhaps the most important.

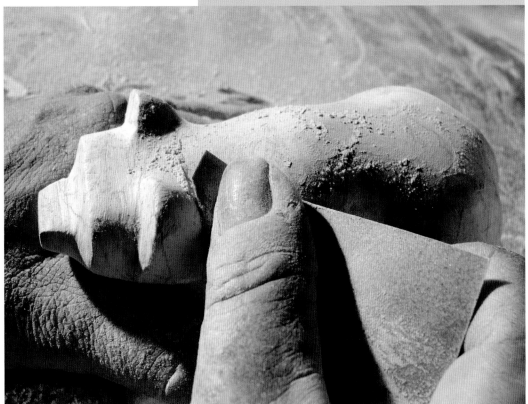

Sanding the standing bear.

Sanding

Beginning with your coarsest sandpaper, 80 grit, fold the paper into a triangle to better sand corners and angles.

Begin with the top of the head. Working slowly and carefully, sand the whole piece. With the 80 grit, being the coarsest sandpaper, notice how quickly so many of the tool marks are eliminated. Use sweeping motions.

Periodically brush off your piece so that you can see the tool marks that you want to eliminate.

See the sanded strip as compared to the sides of the bear.

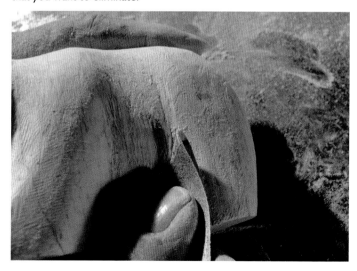

With the folded angle, sand the crease of the legs.

Don't apply too much pressure; let the sandpaper do the work.

Sand the belly…

…carefully work the ears.

80 grit will eliminate a lot of your rasp marks, but will create marks of its own. These marks will be eliminated with the finer sandpapers.

Sand the forehead and snout carefully…

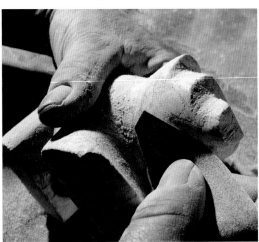

…then under the chin…

…and the edges of the nose…

…then get rid of the dust and take a look at your piece to evaluate how much more sanding needs to be done with the 80 grit.

Notice how some of the deep tool marks are almost gone.

Continue sanding the deeper apparent tool marks.

At this point, if most of the sanding marks on your bear are just those created by the 80 grit sandpaper, switch to the 120 grit.

Sand the entire piece, removing the 80 grit marks.

Notice how much smoother the bear is becoming.

The 220 grit will remove the marks left behind by the 120 grit sandpaper.

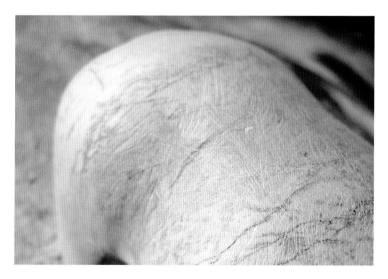

Notice how the front of the piece has the 80 grit sanding marks while the back of the bear is smoother due to the 120 grit sanding.

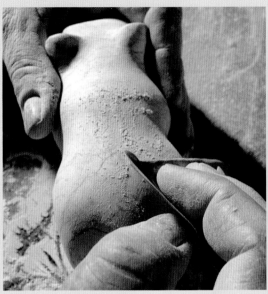

Once you have sanded the entire piece with the 120 grit sandpaper, switch over to the 220.

Again, you can go up to 800 grit if you want from this point on.

Sanding takes time, be patient.

Don't forget to sand all the way to the edges and base of the bear.

Take a look at your piece and look for areas you may not be happy with…

Notice how smooth the bear is becoming.

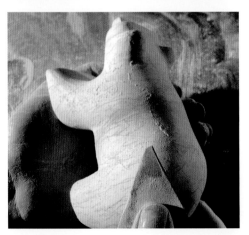

Now that the sanding is near completion, you can see the color of the stone begin to show.

Pay attention to small areas such as the front of the ears.

Be careful with the snout.

...and re-sand them.

Once you are satisfied with your sanding, wipe off the bear or run it under water to remove all the dust.

Your bear should look something like this.

Polishing

Now you will be creating a smooth finish with steel wool before applying the polish of your choice. The steel wool will remove any and all blemishes, file marks, and will achieve an even smoother finish. We suggest 0000 steel wool. As far as the polish goes, what you use depends on the look you want. When using oil finishes you need to realize that oils are affected by sunlight, heat, and the simple acidity in human skin. Oiled pieces dull and need re-polishing at some point. However, many folks want to use natural products, so using tung oil, linseed oil, or beeswax is all they will consider (other oils are okay as well, such as olive oil, etc.). Professionals tend to use clear spray enamel in place of oils because they do not have to worry about re-oiling. Clear spray enamels come in either gloss or satin finishes depending on the look they want to achieve. We chose to use a combination of carnuba and beeswax (or in simple words, an oil finish).

Polishing the standing bear.

Throughout the book you have been instructed not to apply too much pressure when carving. However, when finishing with steel wool, you want to do just the opposite. You want to apply pressure as you smooth with the steel wool.

A note of caution: remember to have a firm grip on your piece and work delicately around the head.

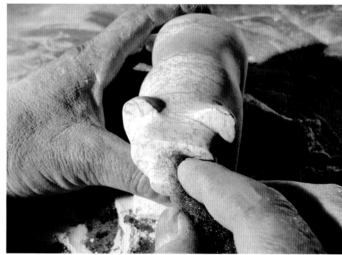

Notice the smoothness we have achieved with the 0000 steel wool.

When you are satisfied with the finish, get the polish of your choice. In this case, we are using an oil polish. Clean your bear before applying the polish to the piece. You can do so by either wiping it off with a damp cloth or running it under water. The piece must be completely dry before applying any finish (minimum 1 hour drying time).

We used an oil based polish applied to a cloth. See how the colors are jumping out of the stone where the polish has been applied.

If you using an oil based polish, it will appear high gloss at first, however it will eventually absorb into the stone and have a more matt finish.

Congratulations! You have completed your standing bear sculpture!

Bear Pattern

Patterns to use on a block or raw piece of soapstone. We recommend that you make copies of the patterns before cutting them out.

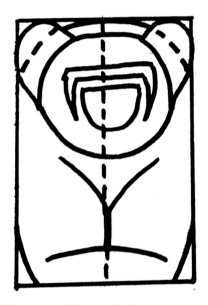

Front view of the standing bear pattern.

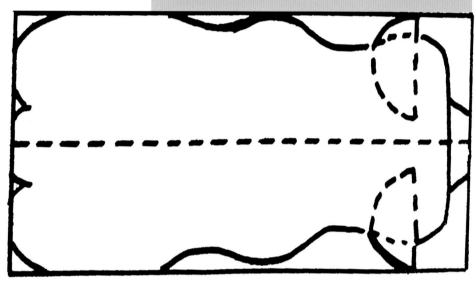

Top view of the standing bear pattern.

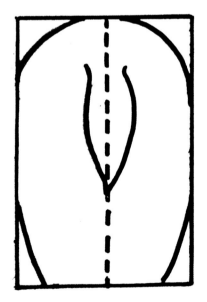

Back view of the standing bear pattern.

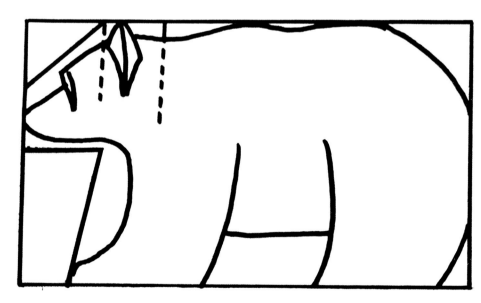

Side view of the standing bear pattern.

Gallery

Some examples of Dawn Hartwig's art.

Flower pot by Dawn Hartwig

Horse by Dawn Hartwig.

Bear by Dawn Hartwig.

Horse heads by Dawn Hartwig